Table of Contents

Catholic Reflections Book C
Item #622, ISBN 978-1-934732-12-0

by Jennifer Schweighofer & Kelly Gilbert

Nihil Obstat	Imprimatur	The *nihil obstat* and *imprimatur* are official declarations that the material
Reverend J. Brian Bransfield	Cardinal Justin Rigali	reviewed is free of doctrinal and moral error. No implication is contained
August 29, 2011	Archbishop of Philadelphia	therein that those who gave the *nihil obstat* and *imprimatur* agree with
	September 5, 2011	the contents, opinions, or statements expressed.

Scripture quotations in this publication are from the Contemporary English Version,
Copyright © 1991, 1992, 1995 by American Bible Society. Used by permission.

My Catholic Life

Finish the sentences.

My name is...

_____

- -

_____

_____

I am a...

Catholic

_____

The name of my church is...

_____

- -

_____

_____

The name of my priest is...

_____

- -

_____

_____

The name of my bishop or archbishop is...

_____

- -

_____

_____

The name of the pope is...

_____

- -

_____

_____

One person who helps me learn about being Catholic is...

_____

- -

_____

The Good I Will Do!

Think about the good you can do in the world this school year. Draw a picture to show how you can take care of God's creation, help someone in need, teach others about God, or do something else good.

Finish the sentence: **This year, I will try to...**

Jesus, Son of God

Read

Jesus is the Son of God. He was born of the Virgin Mary. Jesus is both human and divine. God wanted the world to know how much he loves us. God was sad that the world was full of sin. He wanted us to learn how to live his way. God sent Jesus to live on earth to be our role model. Jesus died on the cross to save all of us from sin.

Talk About It!

What do you think Jesus was like when he was your age?

Reflection Words

Jesus   Son of God

human   divine   role model

Explore   Number the events of Jesus' life in the correct order.

Crucifixion

Jesus at the Temple

Nativity

Ascension

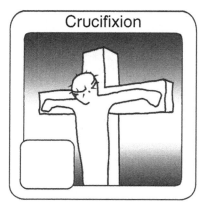

Jesus' Baptism

Resurrection

Reflect   Why is Jesus special to you?

Step 1: Write some words that describe Jesus.

Step 2: Describe why Jesus is special to you.

Work of Jesus

Read

Jesus loved God very much. He wanted people to know how much God loved them. Jesus taught others how to live God's way. He showed them how to live so they could go to heaven. Jesus tried to be a friend to everyone. He helped people who were in need. He taught people how to pray. He healed the sick. He even performed miracles!

Talk About It!

Think of one of Jesus' miracles. What makes this a miracle?

Reflection Words

Jesus   love   heaven   friend
help   pray   heal   miracle

Explore Follow in Jesus' footsteps! Write a word in each footprint that tells how you can be like Jesus.

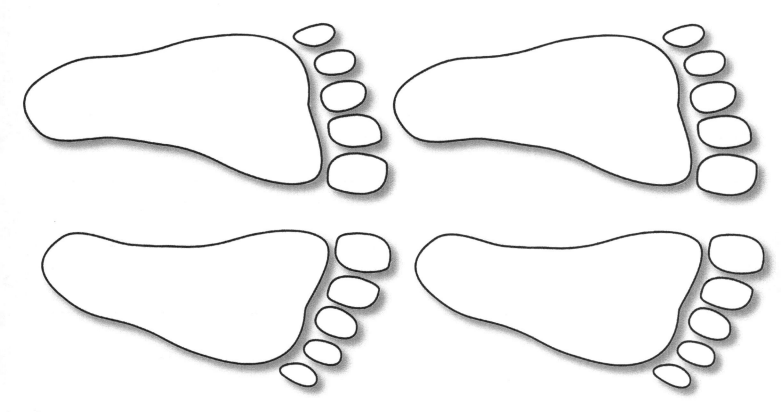

Reflect   What does Jesus teach you about helping others?

Step 1: Draw a picture of how you can help others.

Step 2: Describe how Jesus teaches you about helping others.

Jesus Teaches Us How to Love

Read

Jesus teaches us how to love. This is an important lesson! Jesus loves all people. He does not love a person more or less because he or she is different. Jesus loves everyone, from unborn babies to very old people. In the two Great Commandments, Jesus tells us how to love: "Love the Lord your God with all your heart, soul, and mind... Love others as much as you love yourself." (Matthew 22: 37, 39)

Talk About It!

Besides the two Great Commandments, how does Jesus teach us about love?

Reflection Words

Jesus   teach   love

Great Commandments

Explore

Matthew 7:12 says, "Treat others as you want them to treat you." This saying has a special name. Use the code to find out what it is! On each line, write the letter that goes with that number.

D	G	P	O	H	L	U	M	E	R	T	N
1	2	3	4	5	6	7	8	9	10	11	12

___ ___ ___
11 5   9

___ ___ ___ ___ ___ ___
2   4   6   1   9   12

___ ___ ___ ___
10 7   6   9

Reflect What can you do to follow Jesus' two Great Commandments?

Step 1: Draw something you can do to follow Jesus' two Great Commandments.

Step 2: Describe how you can follow Jesus' two Great Commandments.

God's Ten Commandments

Read

God gave us rules that he wants us to live by. These rules are called the Ten Commandments. He gave us these commandments because he loves us. He wants to help us live holy lives. If we break one of God's commandments, it is a sin. This makes God very sad, because it means that we do not want to be close to him. When we follow the Ten Commandments, God is happy. It means we choose to live his way.

Talk About It!

Who can help you follow the Ten Commandments?

Reflection Words

rules   Ten Commandments

holy   sin   follow   choose

Explore   Number the Ten Commandments in the correct order.

_____ Remember to keep holy the Sabbath day.

_____ You shall not commit adultery.

_____ I am the Lord your God; you shall not have strange gods before me.

_____ You shall not want to take your neighbor's possessions.

_____ You shall not kill.

_____ Honor your father and your mother.

_____ You shall not misuse the name of the Lord your God.

_____ You shall not want to take your neighbor's wife or husband.

_____ You shall not tell lies against your neighbor.

_____ You shall not steal.

Reflect
Write a new commandment that kids should follow at school.

Step 1: Write your new commandment on the stone tablet.

Step 2: Write about why your new commandment is important for kids to follow.

Sacraments

Read

A sacrament is a sign of Jesus' presence in our lives. Jesus gave us seven sacraments to show us he is always with us. The sacraments give us grace and help us live God's way. There are seven sacraments:

Baptism • Reconciliation • Holy Eucharist • Confirmation
Matrimony • Holy Orders • Anointing of the Sick

Talk About It!

How do the sacraments help us live a holy life?

Reflection Words

sacrament   sign   grace

Explore   Find the words in the puzzle below. Circle the words.

BAPTISM   RECONCILIATION   EUCHARIST
CONFIRMATION   HOLY ORDERS   MATRIMONY   ANOINT

B	G	C	O	N	F	I	R	M	A	T	I	O	N	D
A	W	N	T	L	O	B	C	P	N	E	V	X	R	U
P	L	Q	B	A	H	O	L	Y	O	R	D	E	R	S
T	M	Y	N	T	K	T	F	C	I	K	W	N	H	Z
I	G	O	A	I	A	J	P	T	N	V	G	A	J	A
S	E	U	C	H	A	R	I	S	T	X	A	H	E	M
M	A	T	R	I	M	O	N	Y	L	Z	V	H	C	B
R	E	C	O	N	C	I	L	I	A	T	I	O	N	Q

Reflect   Describe a sacrament that you have received.

Step 1: Draw a picture of yourself receiving one of the sacraments.

Step 2: Describe what happens during this sacrament.

Sacramentals

Read

Sacramentals are special objects that have been blessed by the Church. They help us celebrate the sacraments. Holy water and candles are sacramentals. So are rosaries and crucifixes.

Prayers and blessings can be sacramentals, too. The Sign of the Cross is one of the most important sacramentals because it reminds us of Jesus' love for us.

Talk About It!

What sacramentals do you have in your house? How are they used?

Reflection Words

sacramental   object   celebrate
prayer   blessing   rosary
crucifix   Sign of the Cross

Explore   Draw a line from each word to the correct sacramental.

Holy Water •

Candle •

Prayer •

Crucifix •

Rosary •

Reflect What is your favorite sacramental?

Step 1: Draw a picture of your favorite sacramental.

Step 2: Describe your favorite sacramental and explain why it is your favorite.

Prayer

Read

Prayer is talking to God. When we pray to God, we also listen to him. We pray for many reasons. We pray to tell God we love him. We pray to praise God. We pray to thank God for all he does for us. We pray to ask God's forgiveness when we sin. We pray to ask God to help others. We can pray anytime, anywhere. We can pray alone or with others. We can pray out loud or in the quiet of our hearts!

Talk About It!

How often should we pray to God?

Reflection Words

prayer   talking   listen   love

praise   thank   ask   help

Explore   Draw a picture or write about how you feel...

...before you pray.	...while you pray.	...after you pray.

Reflect   Complete each sentence to make a prayer.

God, I love you because...

God, I praise you for...

God, thank you for...

God, I am sorry for...

God, please help...

Sin

Read

When we sin, we make a choice to disobey God. Sin causes us to do hurtful things to ourselves and others. There are two types of sin: venial sin and mortal sin. Venial sins make God sad. We commit venial sins when we say hurtful things or when we choose to disobey our parents. Mortal sins are very bad sins, such as killing. These sins take away our friendship with God. All sin hurts God because he wants us to live holy lives. Always try to avoid sin and live God's way!

Talk About It!

What should we do if we sin?

Who can help us avoid sin?

Reflection Words

sin   choice   disobey

venial sin   mortal sin

Explore Follow the good paths to find Jesus. Avoid the sinful paths!

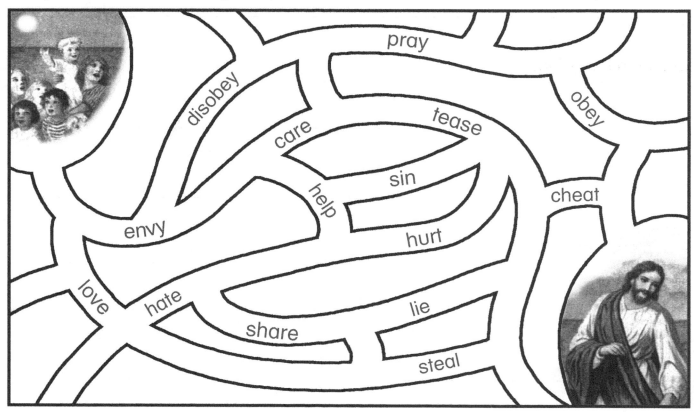

Reflect How does sin hurt our friendship with God? How can we fix this friendship?

Step 1: Write some words to describe how God feels when we sin.

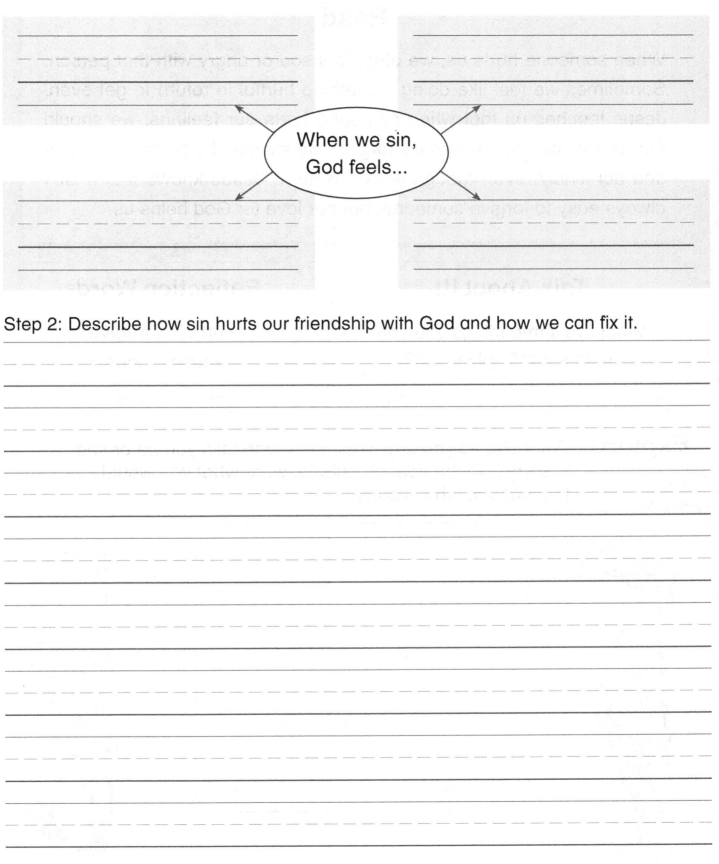

When we sin,
God feels...

Step 2: Describe how sin hurts our friendship with God and how we can fix it.

Forgiveness

Read

When someone hurts us, we often feel sad or angry with that person. Sometimes we feel like doing something hurtful in return to get even. Jesus teaches us that when someone hurts our feelings, we should forgive that person. When we forgive, we excuse the person's actions and act kindly, even though we were hurt. Jesus knows that it isn't always easy to forgive someone, but our love for God helps us.

Talk About It!

What are some things you can do to show forgiveness?

Reflection Words

hurtful   forgive
excuse   kindly

Explore   What should you say when someone tells you he or she is sorry? In the speech bubble, write what you would say to someone who is sorry.

Reflect Write your own prayer to tell God you are sorry and ask his forgiveness.

Step 1: Draw a picture of how you feel when you are sorry.

Step 2: Write your own prayer. Explain why you are sorry and ask God to forgive you.

Act of Contrition

Read

The Act of Contrition is a prayer that we say to tell God we are sorry. This prayer tells God that we regret our sins, that we wish to make up for them, and that we will try not to sin again. We say this prayer when we receive the Sacrament of Reconciliation. We can also say this prayer any time we want to tell God we are sorry for hurting our friendship with him.

Talk About It!

When might you say this prayer other than during confession?

Reflection Words

prayer   contrition
sorry   regret

Explore Write the correct words to complete the Act of Contrition.

penance	love	mercy	sorry

My God, I am __1__ for my sins with all my heart. In choosing to do wrong and failing to do good, I have sinned against you whom I should __2__ above all things. I firmly intend, with your help, to do __3__, to sin no more, and to avoid whatever leads me to sin. Our Savior Jesus Christ suffered and died for us. In his name, my God have __4__. Amen.

1. _____

2. _____

3. _____

4. _____

Reflect
Draw a picture to tell God you are sorry.
Include a note telling him why you are sorry.

Mary, Mother of Jesus

Read

Mary is the Mother of Jesus. She is also our Mother and the Mother of the Church. She has very special grace from God! We look to Mary as our model of how to live and be closer to God. When the angel Gabriel told Mary God's plan, Mary said that she would do as God asked. She teaches us how to trust and obey God, as she trusted him and obeyed him.

Talk About It!

How do you think Mary felt when Gabriel told her God's plan?

Reflection Words

Mary   Mother   grace
model   Gabriel

Explore Write the words. Color the picture of Mary.

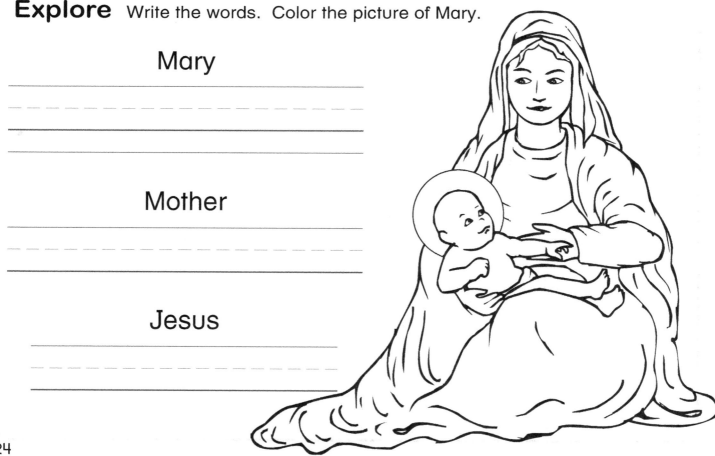

Mary

_____

_____

Mother

_____

_____

Jesus

_____

_____

Reflect Why is Mary our model of how to live.

Step 1: Write some words to describe Mary.

Step 2: Describe why Mary is our model of how to live.

Joseph

The angel said, "Joseph, the baby that Mary will have is from the Holy Spirit."
(Matthew 1:20)

Read

Joseph was Mary's husband and Jesus' foster father. He worked as a carpenter. Together, Joseph, Mary, and Jesus are called the Holy Family. Joseph became a saint because he was a very good man who trusted in God. When you pray, thank Saint Joseph for being a guardian to Mary and Jesus.

Talk About It!

What does it mean to be a foster father?

Reflection Words

Joseph   husband   foster father
Holy Family   saint   guardian

Explore   Joseph was a carpenter. Circle the things he may have built.

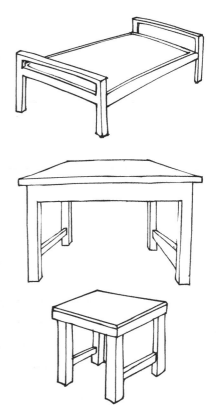

Reflect   How did Joseph show his trust in God?

Step 1: Draw a picture of the Holy Family.

Step 2: Describe how Joseph showed that he trusted God.

Advent

Read

Advent is a special time of waiting and preparing. It is the four-week season before Christmas. During Advent, we get ready to celebrate the birth of Jesus. We prepare our hearts to welcome him into our lives. Advent is celebrated with a wreath of four candles. One candle is pink and the others are violet. A new candle is lit each week to celebrate the coming of Christ.

Talk About It!

What is something your family does during Advent?

Reflection Words

Advent   prepare   season
celebrate   Jesus   candle   wreath

Explore

Write six words that describe Advent.

1 _____

2 _____

3 _____

4 _____

5 _____

6 _____

Reflect   Draw a welcome sign for Jesus to show him you are excited for his arrival!

Write one sentence about why Advent is important.

Christmas Day

Read

On Christmas Day, we celebrate the birth of Jesus. He was born in the town of Bethlehem. The inn was full, so Mary and Joseph had to stay in the stables with the animals. This is where Jesus was born! They had no crib for Jesus, so they put him in a manger. A manger is used to hold food for barn animals. Many people came to visit baby Jesus. They brought him gifts such as gold, myrrh, and frankincense.

Talk About It!

How do you celebrate Christmas Day?

Reflection Words

Christmas Day   Jesus   Bethlehem   manger   myrrh   frankincense

Explore   Write the words. Match each word correctly to the Nativity.

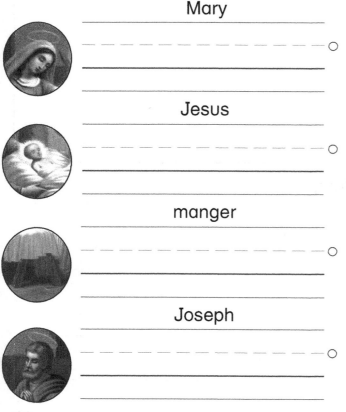

Mary
_____
- - - - - - - - - - - - - - - ○
_____

Jesus
_____
- - - - - - - - - - - - - - - ○
_____

manger
_____
- - - - - - - - - - - - - - - ○
_____

Joseph
_____
- - - - - - - - - - - - - - - ○
_____

Reflect   What gift would you give Jesus for his birthday? Why?

Step 1: Draw a picture of a gift you would give Jesus.

Step 2: Describe the gift you would give Jesus. Why would you give him this gift?

The Holy Trinity

I pray that the Lord Jesus Christ will bless you....May God bless you...
and may the Holy Spirit join all your hearts together. (2 Corinthians 13:13)

Read

The Holy Trinity is three divine persons in one God: God, the Father; Jesus, the Son; and the Holy Spirit. Each person in the Holy Trinity has a special job! God is our Creator. Jesus is our Savior. The Holy Spirit guides us and gives us grace. The Sign of the Cross and Glory Be are prayers about the Holy Trinity.

Talk About It!

When do we say the Sign of the Cross?
When do we say the Glory Be?

Reflection Words

Holy Trinity   Father
Son   Holy Spirit   grace

Explore   Draw a line from the words on the left to the correct person.

Our Creator •
Our Savior •
Our Guide •

Write the words **Creator**, **Savior**, and **Guide**.

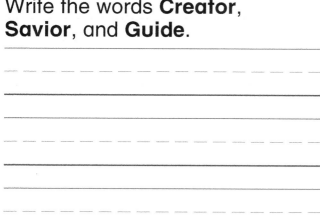

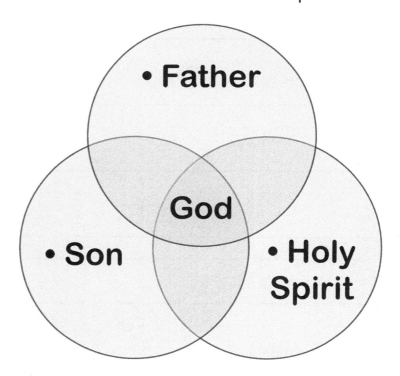

Reflect   Why is the Holy Trinity so important to our faith?

Step 1: Draw a picture of the Holy Trinity.

Step 2: Describe why the Holy Trinity is so important to our faith.

The Bible

Read

The Bible is a very special book. It is also called Sacred Scripture. The stories in the Bible are the Word of God. God chose people and inspired them to write the stories we find in the Bible. The Bible has two parts. The first part is the Old Testament. It is about the world before Jesus was born. The second part is the New Testament. It is about the birth, life, and death of Jesus.

Talk About It!

What do we learn from the stories in the Bible?

Reflection Words

Bible   Word of God   inspire

Sacred Scripture   Old Testament

New Testament

Explore

Draw a line from each book on the left to the correct part of the Bible on the right.

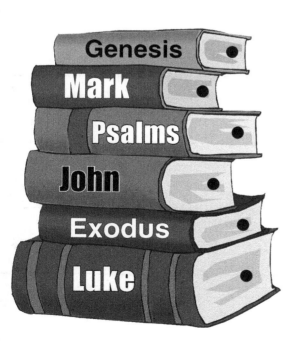

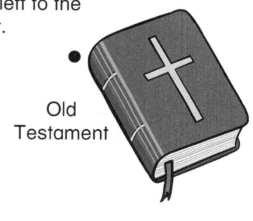

Old Testament

New Testament

Reflect   What is your favorite Bible story?

Step 1: Draw pictures of the beginning, middle, and end of your favorite Bible story.

Beginning	Middle	End

Step 2: Describe your favorite Bible story. What is the lesson in this story?

_____

_____

_____

_____

_____

_____

_____

_____

_____

_____

_____

_____

The Old Testament

Read

The Old Testament is the first part of the Bible. There are 46 books in the Old Testament. These books help us learn about the history of the world before Jesus was born. In the Old Testament, we read the story of creation. We also meet leaders of God's people, such as Abraham, Moses, and Noah. The Old Testament is important because it tells us about God's promise to his people and his great love for us.

Talk About It!

What are some books from the Old Testament? What stories are told in these books?

Reflection Words

Old Testament   history

leaders   promise

Explore   Unscramble the Old Testament book names.

Genesis   Numbers   Judges   Ruth   Proverbs   Exodus

s e s e G i n

_ _ _ _ _ _ _

d u s J e g

_ _ _ _ _ _

u s o d x E

_ _ _ _ _ _

m e N u b s r

_ _ _ _ _ _ _

u R t h

_ _ _ _

P o s r b e v r

_ _ _ _ _ _ _ _

Reflect   Who do you think is the most important character in the Old Testament?

Step 1: Draw a picture of a character from the Old Testament.

Step 2: Describe this character. What did this character do that was important?

The Book of Genesis

Read

The first book in the Old Testament is the Book of Genesis. The Book of Genesis tells us the story of creation. We learn how God created everything from nothing, and that he did this out of love. We also read the story of Adam and Eve. When Adam and Eve disobeyed God, it was the first sin. This is called original sin. Ever since then, all humans have been born sinful.

Talk About It!

Why are all humans born with original sin?

Reflection Words

Genesis   creation
Adam   Eve   original sin

Explore   Write the words. Match the words to the correct picture.

Garden of Eden •

_____

_____

Serpent •

_____

_____

Adam and Eve •

_____

_____

Reflect   What do we learn in the Book of Genesis?

Step 1: Write three things we learn in the Book of Genesis.

1

2

3

Step 2: Write a paragraph about what we learn in the Book of Genesis.

The Book of Exodus

Read

The second book in the Old Testament is the Book of Exodus. This book tells us the story of Moses. We learn that God chose Moses to lead the Hebrews out of Egypt. After Moses freed the Hebrews, God called Moses to Mount Sinai. He gave Moses the Ten Commandments. God made a covenant with the Hebrews. He promised that if they followed his commandments, he would give them the land of Canaan.

Talk About It!

What is a covenant? Why did God make a covenant with the Hebrews?

Reflection Words

Exodus   Moses

Hebrews   covenant

Explore   Follow Moses to the promised land of Canaan!

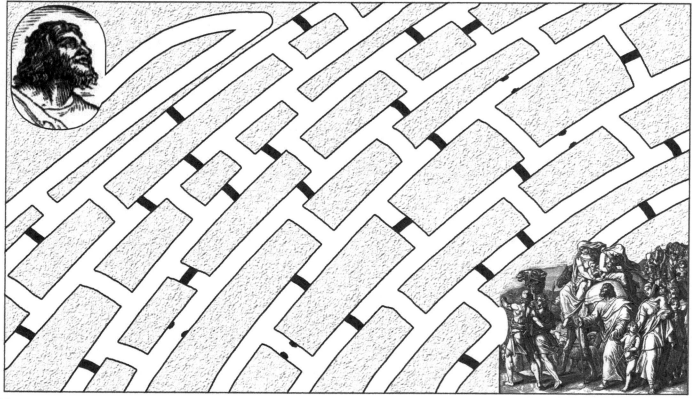

Reflect   Why do you think God chose Moses to lead the Hebrews out of Egypt?

Step 1: Write some words to describe Moses.

Step 2: Describe why you think God chose Moses to lead the Hebrews out of Egypt.

The New Testament

Read

The second part of the Bible is called the New Testament. In the New Testament, there are 27 books. These books show us how to live God's way. We learn about how God fulfills his promise to his people through his Son. The New Testament helps us learn about the beginning of our Church. It also tells us about Jesus and the great things he did while he was on earth.

Talk About It!

What are some books from the New Testament? What stories are told in these books?

Reflection Words

New Testament
fulfill   promise

Explore   Color the books of the New Testament.

Matthew

Mark

Luke

John

Acts

Romans

1 Corinthians

2 Corinthians

Galatians

Ephesians

Philippians

Colossians

1 Thessalonians

2 Thessalonians

1 Timothy

2 Timothy

Titus

Philemon

Hebrews

James

1 Peter

2 Peter

1 John

2 John

3 John

Jude

Revelation

Reflect   What does the New Testament teach us about Jesus?

Step 1: Write three things the New Testament teaches us about Jesus.

1

2

3

Step 2: Write a paragraph about what the New Testament teaches us about Jesus.

The Gospels

Read

The Gospels are the first four books in the New Testament. The word "gospel" means "good news." The good news is all about Jesus! The Gospels are the books of Matthew, Mark, Luke, and John. Each book tells a story about Jesus in its own way. The Gospels teach us about the things Jesus did on earth. They show us how he was a teacher, healer, and friend. The Gospels also tell us the story of Jesus' death. We read from the Gospels every time we celebrate Mass!

Talk About It!

What is the "good news" we learn about in the Gospels?

Reflection Words

Gospel   good news   Matthew
Mark   Luke   John

Explore

Write the names of the Gospels.
Connect each name to the correct symbol.

Matthew •

_____

_____

Mark •

_____

_____

Luke •

_____

_____

John •

_____

Reflect   What is the good news we learn about in the Gospels?

Step 1: Draw a picture of the good news we learn about in the Gospels.

Step 2: Describe the good news we learn about in the Gospels.

The Catholic Church

Read

The Catholic Church is a sign of God's love for us. It was started many years ago by Jesus. We become part of the Catholic Church when we are baptized. People who belong to the Catholic Church are called Catholics. Just like Jesus, Catholics want everyone to love God! Jesus chose Saint Peter to be the first leader of the Church. Today, we call the leader of the Church the pope. The pope lives in Vatican City in Rome.

Talk About It!

How is the Catholic Church a sign of God's love for us?

Reflection Words

Catholic Church   Saint Peter
Jesus   Catholics   pope
Vatican City

Explore   Draw a picture of the current pope. What is his name?

Reflect   Write a word or phrase for each letter to describe what "Catholic" means.

C _____

A _____

T _____

H _____

O _____

L _____

I _____

C _____

What does being Catholic mean to you?

_____

_____

_____

_____

_____

_____

Respecting Other Religions

Read

God wants us to respect all people. God made everyone special.
No two people are the same! Some people might speak a different
language or wear different clothes. Others may belong to a different
religion. There are many people in the world who are not Catholic.
They might show their love for God in a different way than we do.
Some people may not know about Jesus. We may be different, but
God still wants us to show respect for one another!

Talk About It!

What are some other religions? What makes
them different from the Catholic faith?

Reflection Words

faith   religion

Catholic   respect

Explore Connect each religion to the correct symbol.

Catholic   Islam   Hindu   Jewish

•   •   •   •

•   •   •   •

Reflect   How can you show respect for people of other religions?

Step 1: Write three things you can do to show respect for people of other religions.

1

2

3

Step 2: Write a paragraph about how you can show respect for people of other religions.

The Last Supper

Read

The Last Supper is the last meal that Jesus and the apostles had together before Jesus' death. Before they began eating, Jesus washed the feet of each of the apostles. Then, he prepared some bread and wine. He told the apostles that each time they celebrated Holy Communion, they would be reminded of Jesus' love. Today, we are still reminded of Jesus' love. Each time we celebrate Mass, the Eucharist lets us know that Jesus is still with us.

Talk About It!

Why do you think Jesus washed the apostles' feet?

Reflection Words

Last Supper   Jesus   apostles
bread and wine   Eucharist

Explore   Fill in the missing letters to complete the apostles' names.

P___il___p

___o___n

An___re___

Ja___e___

P___te___

B___rtholo___ew

1. Peter
2. Andrew
3. James
4. John
5. Philip
6. Bartholomew
7. Thomas
8. Matthew
9. James
10. Thaddaeus
11. Simon
12. Judas

M___tt___ew

___hom___s

Ju___a___

___am___s

T___ad___aeus

Si___o___

Reflect   What do you think it would have been like to be at the Last Supper?

Step 1: Write six adjectives or adverbs to describe the Last Supper.

① _____

④ _____

② _____

⑤ _____

③ _____

⑥ _____

Step 2: Describe what you think it would have been like to be at the Last Supper.

_____

_____

_____

_____

_____

_____

_____

_____

_____

_____

_____

Holy Week

Jesus then said, "I am the one who raises the dead to life! Everyone who has faith in me will live, even if they die..." (John 11:25)

Read

Holy Week is celebrated during the last week of Lent. During this week, we remember the life and death of Jesus. Holy Week begins on Palm Sunday and ends on Holy Saturday. Triduum takes place during Holy Week and includes Holy Thursday evening, Good Friday, Holy Saturday, and Easter Sunday.

Talk About It!

How do we celebrate each day of Holy Week?

Reflection Words

Holy Week   Lent
Palm Sunday   Triduum

Explore   Write the days of Holy Week in the correct order.

Good Friday   Holy Thursday

Palm Sunday   Holy Saturday

1. _____

2. _____

3. _____

4. _____

Reflect
What is your favorite part about celebrating Holy Week?

Step 1: Draw a picture of something your family does to celebrate Holy Week.

Step 2: Describe your favorite part of celebrating Holy Week.

My First Confession

Read

When we act in a way that hurts God and others, we need to say we are sorry. We celebrate the Sacrament of Reconciliation to confess our sins and ask for God's forgiveness.

The priest gives us acts of penance to make up for our sins. God always loves us, even when we sin. If we are truly sorry for our sins, God will always forgive us.

Talk About It!

What are some acts of penance you can do to make up for your sins?

Reflection Words

Sacrament of Reconciliation
confess   forgiveness
penance

Explore

Below are some things that happen during confession. Number them in the correct order.

_____ You say the Act of Contrition.

_____ The priest gives you your penance.

_____ You tell the priest how long it has been since your last confession.

_____ The priest absolves your sins.

_____ You tell the priest your sins.

Reflect   Why is it important to confess your sins?

Step 1: Draw a picture of your first confession.

Step 2: Describe why it is important to confess your sins.

Easter Sunday & the Ascension

Read

Jesus died on the cross to save us from sin. Three days after his death, Jesus rose again. This is called the Resurrection of Jesus. We celebrate this happy event on Easter Sunday.

Forty days after the Resurrection, Jesus returned to heaven to be with God. We call this event the Ascension, and we celebrate it on Ascension Thursday.

Talk About It!

What do the words "resurrection" and "ascension" mean?

Reflection Words

Easter Sunday   Ascension
Resurrection of Jesus
heaven   Ascension Thursday

Explore Compare and contrast Jesus' Resurrection and Ascension.

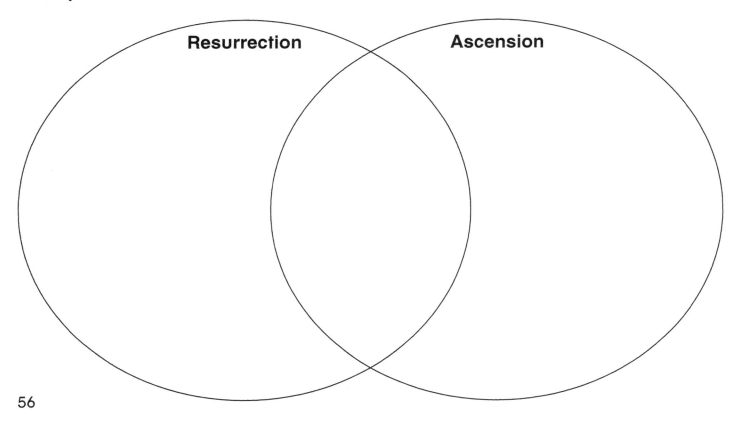

Resurrection

Ascension

Reflect   Describe Jesus' Resurrection or Ascension.

Step 1: Circle the event you chose. Write one word in each box to describe the event.

Resurrection Ascension	④
①	⑤
②	⑥
③	⑦

Step 2: Use your notes to write a paragraph about the event you chose.

_____

_____

_____

_____

_____

_____

_____

_____

_____

_____

_____

My First Holy Communion

Read

Jesus shares himself with us in a special way through the Sacrament of Holy Eucharist. This sacrament is also called the Blessed Sacrament or Holy Communion. During Mass, bread and wine are turned into the Body and Blood of Jesus. Jesus shares this meal with us just as he shared himself with the apostles at the Last Supper. This sacrament brings us closer to Christ and reminds us of his sacrifice.

Talk About It!

Why do you think Jesus shares himself with us through Holy Eucharist?

Reflection Words

Holy Eucharist   Holy Communion
Blessed Sacrament
bread and wine   Body and Blood

Explore

Read the words. Draw a line from each word to the correct dot on the pictures. More than one word may go to the same dot!

paten •

chalice •

bread •

wine •

Body •

Blood •

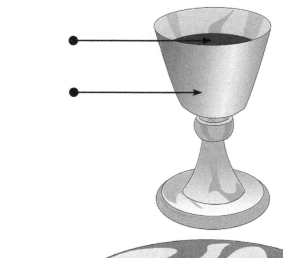

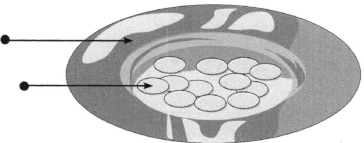

Reflect   Draw a picture of what you think your first Holy Communion will be like.

What is one question you have about your first Holy Communion?

Virtues

Virtues are good habits that help us live holy lives. If we practice these habits, they slowly become part of who we are. Three very special virtues are faith, hope, and love. Faith lets us believe in God, even though we cannot see him. Hope reminds us that God has a plan for each of us. Love is the greatest virtue! God wants us to love him, and to love each other. Love lets us treat others with kindness and respect.

Talk About It!

What are some virtues besides faith, hope, and love?

Reflection Words

virtue	habit	holy
faith	hope	love

Explore   Circle the words that are virtues.

happy   **thankful**   **fair**   honest

`respectful`   **amazed**   *kind*

excited   **patient**

Write these three very special virtues:

faith   **hope**   **love**

_____   _____   _____

_____   _____   _____

_____   _____   _____

Reflect   Describe one of your virtues. Why is this virtue important?

Step 1: Finish each sentence.

One of my virtues is...	I use this virtue to...

This virtue means...

This virtue is important because...

Step 2: Write a paragraph using your notes in Step 1.

_____

- -

_____

- -

_____

- -

_____

- -

_____

- -

_____

- -

_____

- -

_____

- -

_____

Caring for Myself

Read

God created every person in his image. He also made each of us
unique, which means we are each different and special. Our bodies,
hearts, and minds are special gifts from God. Just as God loves us
and cares for us, he wants us to care for ourselves, too. He wants us
to do things that keep us healthy and safe. He also wants us to avoid
things that can make us sick or hurt us.

Talk About It!

Why does God want us to take
good care of ourselves?

Reflection Words

image   unique
care   healthy   safe

Explore Color all the pictures. Circle the ones of people caring for themselves.
Put an "X" on the pictures of people not taking care of themselves.

exercising

no seat belt

brushing
teeth

no helmet

CLICK!
seat belt

eating junk food

Reflect What can you do to take good care of yourself?

Step 1: Draw three things you can do to care for yourself.

Step 2: Describe what you can do to take good care of yourself.

The Liturgical Year

Read

The Liturgical Year is made up of special seasons that the Church celebrates. It is also called the Church Year. The seasons of the Liturgical Year are Advent, Christmas, Ordinary Time, Lent, Triduum, and Easter. Each season is celebrated with special colors and feast days. The liturgical seasons help us remember different events in Jesus' life.

Talk About It!

Which liturgical season do you think is the most important? Why?

Reflection Words

Liturgical Year   Church Year   celebrate
Advent   Christmas   Lent   Triduum
Easter   Ordinary Time   feast day

Explore

Use the code below to color the liturgical wheel.

Color Code

1 = Purple

2 = Green

3 = Red

Why were Easter and Christmas not assigned colors?

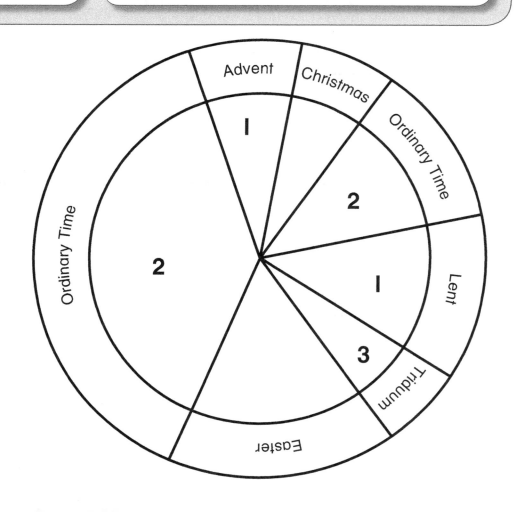

Reflect   Which liturgical season is your favorite? Why?

Step 1: Draw a picture of your favorite liturgical season.

[Empty box for drawing]

Step 2: Describe this liturgical season and why it is your favorite.

Parts of Mass

Jesus answered, "The Scriptures say: `Worship the Lord your God and serve only him!'"
(Luke 4:8)

Read

During Mass, we gather to worship as God's family. We praise God and thank him for his blessings. We also remember God's greatest gift to us: his Son, Jesus. Mass is always celebrated in the same order. There are four parts to Mass: Introductory Rites, Liturgy of the Word, Liturgy of the Eucharist, and Concluding Rite.

Talk About It!

Who are some people who help us celebrate Mass? What are their jobs?

Reflection Words

Mass   gather   worship
Introductory Rites   Liturgy of the Word
Liturgy of the Eucharist   Concluding Rite

Explore   Write or draw one thing that happens during each part of Mass.

Introductory Rites	Liturgy of the Word
Liturgy of the Eucharist	**Concluding Rite**

Reflect   Why is it important to attend Mass?

Step 1: Write three reasons it is important to attend Mass.

1

2

3

Step 2: Use your notes to write a paragraph about why it is important to attend Mass.

Liturgy of the Eucharist

Read

Liturgy of the Eucharist is the third part of Mass. During this time, we remember Jesus' death on the cross. We get ourselves ready to receive Holy Eucharist by preparing the altar and gifts. Then we pray the Eucharistic prayer and the Lord's Prayer. We offer each other the sign of peace. The priest breaks the bread and we receive Holy Communion. To end Liturgy of the Eucharist, we pray silently.

Talk About It!

What is the sign of peace?
Why is this important?

Reflection Words

Liturgy of the Eucharist   altar
pray   sign of peace   communion

Explore   Look at the words in the box. Find the words in the puzzle.

ALTAR   EUCHARIST   PEACE   LITURGY   LORDS PRAYER

L	I	T	U	R	G	Y	W	P	B	Q	L
X	A	E	D	D	F	T	A	E	F	M	D
P	L	O	R	D	S	P	R	A	Y	E	R
S	T	H	M	A	C	A	Q	C	J	O	Y
Y	A	A	K	Z	B	R	S	E	A	E	V
I	R	V	E	U	C	H	A	R	I	S	T

Reflect   What might you pray about after you receive Holy Communion?

Step 1: Write or draw four things you might pray about after you receive Holy Communion.

Step 2: Describe what you might pray about after you receive Holy Communion.

Liturgy of the Word

Read

Liturgy of the Word is the second part of Mass. During this time, we listen to three readings from the Bible. The first reading is from the Old Testament. The second reading is from the New Testament. The third reading is from the Gospels. The readings tell us how to live God's way. We also hear the priest's homily, which helps us to understand God's Word. Finally, we profess our faith and end with intercessions, which are special prayers to God.

Talk About It!

Why do we listen to Bible readings during Mass?

Reflection Words

Liturgy of the Word   readings   homily   profess   intercessions

Explore   Unscramble the words in the boxes to spell the words below.

word   liturgy   Bible   reading   homily   profess

turgliy
__ __ __ __ __ __ __

leBib
__ __ __ __ __

hyomil
__ __ __ __ __ __

neardig
__ __ __ __ __ __ __

orwd
__ __ __ __

froseps
__ __ __ __ __ __ __

Reflect
What is a Bible story that might be read during Liturgy of the Word?

Step 1: Draw a picture of a Bible story that might be read during Liturgy of the Word.

Step 2: Why might this story be read during Liturgy of the Word? What is the story's lesson?

The Apostles' Creed

Read

The Apostles' Creed is a prayer about our Catholic beliefs. Jesus' twelve apostles wrote this prayer many years ago. The Apostles' Creed states that we believe in one true God, honor the life and death of Jesus, and believe in everlasting life.

I believe in God, the Father almighty, Creator of heaven and earth, and in Jesus Christ, his only Son, our Lord, who was conceived by the Holy Spirit, born of the Virgin Mary, suffered under Pontius Pilate, was crucified, died and was buried; he descended into hell; on the third day he rose again from the dead; he ascended into heaven, and is seated at the right hand of God the Father almighty; from there he will come to judge the living and the dead. I believe in the Holy Spirit, the holy catholic Church, the communion of saints, the forgiveness of sins, the resurrection of the body, and life everlasting. Amen.

Talk About It!

Why do we say the Apostles' Creed? When do we say this prayer?

Reflection Words

apostle   creed   beliefs   God   almighty   Jesus

conceived   Holy Spirit   Virgin Mary   suffered   Pontius Pilate

crucified   descended   ascended   communion of saints

forgiveness   resurrection   everlasting

Reflect What is the most important belief stated in the Apostles' Creed?

Step 1: Write some beliefs that are stated in the Apostles' Creed.

Step 2: Choose one belief from your list. Write why you feel it is the most important.

My Ever-Growing Faith

Draw a picture of something that you learned this year about being Catholic.

Finish the sentence: **This year, I learned...**

_____

- -

_____

- -

_____

- -

_____

The Good I Have Done!

Think about the good you have done in the world this school year. Draw a picture to show how you took care of God's creation, helped someone in need, taught others about God, or did something else good.

Finish the sentence: **I did good this year when I...**

_____

_____

_____

_____

_____

_____

My Catholic Prayers & More!

Sign of the Cross
In the name of the Father,
and of the Son, and of
the Holy Spirit.
Amen.

Glory Be
Glory be to the Father, and to the Son,
and to the Holy Spirit, as it was in the
beginning, is now, and will be forever.
Amen.

Angel of God
Angel of God, my guardian dear, to whom God's love commits me here,
ever this day be at my side, to light and guard, to rule and guide. Amen.

Grace Before Meals
Bless us, O Lord,
and these your gifts,
which we are about to receive,
from your bounty,
through Christ our Lord. Amen.

Grace After Meals
We give you thanks, almighty God,
for these and all your gifts which we
have received through Christ our Lord.
Amen.

Morning Prayer
My God, I offer you today,
all I think and do and say,
uniting it with what was done on
Earth by Jesus Christ your Son.

Evening Prayer
Dear God, before I sleep I want to
thank you for this day so full of your
kindness and your joy. I close my
eyes to rest safe in your loving care.

Hail Mary
Hail Mary, full of grace,
the Lord is with thee.
Blessed art thou
among women,
and blessed is the
fruit of thy womb, Jesus.
Holy Mary, Mother of God,
pray for us sinners,
now and at the
hour of our death. Amen.

Our Father
Our Father, who art in heaven,
hallowed be thy name.
Thy kingdom come, thy will be done,
on earth as it is in heaven.
Give us this day our daily bread,
and forgive us our trespasses,
as we forgive those who
trespass against us,
and lead us not into temptation,
but deliver us from evil. Amen.

Simple Act of Faith
Lord, I believe all that you have revealed because you lead us to truth.

Simple Act of Hope
Lord, I place my hope in your promises because you are good and loving.

Simple Act of Love
Lord, I love you with my whole heart, my whole soul, and my whole will.

Act of Contrition

My God, I am sorry for my sins with all my heart.
In choosing to do wrong and failing to do good,
I have sinned against you whom I should love above all things.
I firmly intend, with your help, to do penance, to sin no more,
and to avoid whatever leads me to sin.
Our Savior Jesus Christ suffered and died for us.
In his name, my God, have mercy.

Apostles' Creed

I believe in God, the Father almighty,
Creator of heaven and earth,
and in Jesus Christ, his only Son, our Lord,
who was conceived by the Holy Spirit,
born of the Virgin Mary,
suffered under Pontius Pilate,
was crucified, died and was buried;
he descended into hell;
on the third day he rose again from the dead;
he ascended into heaven,
and is seated at the right hand of God the Father almighty;
from there he will come to judge the living and the dead.
I believe in the Holy Spirit, the holy catholic Church,
the communion of saints, the forgiveness of sins,
the resurrection of the body, and life everlasting. Amen.

The Ten Commandments

1. I am the Lord your God; you shall not have strange gods before me.
2. You shall not take the name of the Lord your God in vain.
3. Remember to keep holy the Lord's Day.
4. Honor your father and mother.
5. You shall not kill.
6. You shall not commit adultery.
7. You shall not steal.
8. You shall not bear false witness against your neighbor.
9. You shall not covet your neighbor's wife.
10. You shall not covet your neighbor's goods.

Jesus' Two Great Commandments

The two commandments that Jesus used to summarize God's Ten Commandments:

1. Love the Lord your God with all your heart, soul, and mind.
2. Love others as much as you love yourself.

My Catholic Words

Advent
The forty days before Christmas when we prepare for the arrival of Jesus Christ.

Ascension
When Jesus returned to heaven to be with God forty days after his Resurrection.

Bible
A book of holy writings about our faith. The Bible is the Word of God. It is also called Sacred Scripture.

Catholic Church
The Church founded by Jesus Christ. Catholics all believe the same faith, worship together, and follow God's laws.

Christmas Day
The day we celebrate the birth of our Lord, Jesus Christ.

Easter Sunday
The day we celebrate the Resurrection of our Lord, Jesus Christ.

Exodus
The second book in the Old Testament. This book tells the story of how Moses helped the Hebrews escape Egypt. It also tells about God's covenant with the Hebrews.

Genesis
The first book in the Old Testament. This book tells the story of creation. It also tells the story of Adam and Eve and the original sin.

Good News
The coming of Jesus Christ to save us from our sins.

Gospels
The first four books of the New Testament: Matthew, Mark, Luke, and John. These books tell us about the good news of Jesus Christ.

Grace
A gift from God that lets us share in his life and helps us to be holy.

Holy Trinity
Three divine persons in one God; the central mystery of the Catholic faith. Also called the Blessed Trinity.

Holy Week
The last week of Lent. Holy Week begins on Palm Sunday and ends on Holy Saturday.

Homily
An explanation of the readings and the Gospel during Liturgy of the Word.

Liturgical Year
Seasons and feasts that we celebrate throughout the year to honor the mystery of Jesus and his life. Also called the Church Year.

Liturgy of the Eucharist
The part of Mass during which we receive the Body and Blood of Jesus Christ.

Liturgy of the Word
The part of Mass during which we listen to Bible readings and the priest's homily.

Mary
Jesus' Mother and our model of faith. She is also known as the Mother of God, the Mother of the Church, and our Blessed Mother.

Mass
The celebration of the Eucharist, during which we gather to pray and give thanks and praise to God.

Mortal Sin
A sin that is very serious and separates us from God.

New Testament
The second part of the Bible; consists of 27 books about how God fulfills his promise to his people through Jesus Christ.

Old Testament
The first part of the Bible; consists of 46 books about God's promise to his people and the history of the world before the birth of Jesus.

Penance
Acts that we do to make up for our sins. A priest gives us penance when we celebrate the Sacrament of Reconciliation.

Pope
The Bishop of Rome and the head of the Catholic Church. The pope carries on the job of Saint Peter, leader of the apostles and the first head of the Church.

Prayer
Talking to and listening to God.

Priest
A man who has received the Sacrament of Holy Orders and leads us in prayer during Mass.

Resurrection of Jesus
When Jesus rose again three days after his death on the cross.

Sacrament
A celebration of God's presence and a sign of Jesus' work. There are seven sacraments: Baptism, Reconciliation, Holy Eucharist, Confirmation, Matrimony, Holy Orders, and the Anointing of the Sick.

Sacrament of Baptism
A sacrament that frees us from sin (including original sin) and makes us members of the Church.

Sacrament of Holy Eucharist
The sacrament in which Jesus shares himself with us. Bread and wine become the Body and Blood of Jesus. Also called the Blessed Sacrament or Holy Communion.

Sacrament of Reconciliation
The sacrament in which we confess our sins and ask for God's forgiveness.

Sacramental
Special signs, actions, and blessings used by the Church to remind us of God's love.

Sacred Scripture
Another name for the Bible; the written Word of God.

Sin
An unholy choice that hurts our relationship with God. *See mortal sin and venial sin.*

Ten Commandments
Ten laws God revealed to Moses, who delivered them to God's chosen people.

Triduum
A period of three special days at the end of Holy Week. It begins on Holy Thursday evening, continues through Good Friday and Holy Saturday, and ends on Easter Sunday. These are the holiest days of the Church year.

Venial sin
A sin that disappoints God, but does not completely separate us from him; less serious than a mortal sin.

Vocation
God's call to serve him through a particular kind of work or service.